The Fox

Suddenly March saw the fox quite near her. He looked up at her and she looked down into his eyes. The fox looked up at her and he knew her. She did not move. The fox knew her and was not afraid.

Everybody knows the two women by their family names. They are March and Banford. They live on a farm together. All they want to do is live on the farm. But then a man comes. He comes to stay, and he likes March. And then there's the fox outside, the dangerous fox. The question for March is this: what do the man and the fox mean for her? This is a love story. But it is not the same as other love stories . . .

D. H. (David Herbert) Lawrence was born in 1885 in Nottinghamshire, England. He came from a working family and was weak and ill as a child.

He wrote a lot about families, and about men and women and their problems. His writing was very new in its time and he could not sell some of his work easily.

In 1912, he met Frieda von Richthofen. She had a husband and children but the two fell in love. They went to live in Germany. They never had any money but lived in different places all over the world. Lawrence was often ill.

His most famous books are *Sons and Lovers* (1913), *The Rainbow* (1915), *Women in Love* (1920) and *Lady Chatterley's Lover* (1928). But he is famous for his stories, too. *The Fox* (1922) was one of these. Lawrence died in 1930.

The following titles are available at Levels 1, 2 and 3:

Level 1
Brown Eyes
Girl Meets Boy
The Hen and the Bull
A Job for Pedro
The Medal of Brigadier Gerard
Run for Your Life
The Streets of London
Surfer!

Level 2
The Birds
Chocky
The Canterville Ghost and the Model
   Millionaire
The Diary
Don't Look Behind You
Don't Look Now
Emily
Flour Babies
The Ghost of Genny Castle
Grandad's Eleven
The Lady in the Lake
Money to Burn
Persuasion
The Railway Children
The Room in the Tower and Other
   Ghost Stories
Simply Suspense
Treasure Island
Under the Greenwood Tree
The Wave   •
We Are All Guilty
The Weirdo

Level 3
Black Beauty
The Black Cat and Other Stories
The Book of Heroic Failures
Calling All Monsters
A Catskill Eagle
Channel Runner
The Darling Buds of May
Dubliners
Earthdark
Forest Gump
The Fugitive
Jane Eyre
King Solomon's Mines
Madame Doubtfire
The Man with Two Shadows and
   Other Ghost Stories
More Heroic Failures
Mrs Dalloway
My Family and Other Animals
Not a Penny More, Not a Penny Less
Rain Man
The Reluctant Queen
Santorini
Sherlock Holmes and the Mystery
   of Boscombe Pool
StarGate
Summer of My German Soldier
The Thirty-nine Steps
Thunder Point
Time Bird
The Turn of the Screw
Twice Shy

For a complete list of the titles available in the Penguin Readers series please write to the following address for a catalogue: Penguin ELT Marketing Department, Penguin Books Ltd, 27 Wrights Lane, London W8 5TZ.

The Fox

D. H. LAWRENCE

Level 2

Retold by Philip Prowse
Series Editor: Derek Strange

PENGUIN BOOKS

PENGUIN BOOKS

Published by the Penguin Group
Penguin Books Ltd, 27 Wrights Lane, London W8 5TZ, England
Penguin Books USA Inc., 375 Hudson Street, New York, New York 10014, USA
Penguin Books Australia Ltd, Ringwood, Victoria, Australia
Penguin Books Canada Ltd, 10 Alcorn Avenue, Toronto, Ontario, Canada M4V 3B2
Penguin Books (NZ) Ltd, 182–190 Wairau Road, Auckland 10, New Zealand

Penguin Books Ltd, Registered Offices: Harmondsworth, Middlesex, England

The Fox first published in 1923
This adaptation published by Penguin Books 1995
5 7 9 10 8 6 4

Copyright © Philip Prowse 1995
Illustrations copyright © Piers Sandford 1995
All rights reserved

The moral right of the adapter and of the illustrator has been asserted

Illustrations by Piers Sandford

Printed in England by Clays Ltd, St Ives plc
Set in 11/14pt Lasercomp Bembo by
Datix International Limited, Bungay, Suffolk

To the teacher:

In addition to all the language forms of Level One, which are used again at this level of the series, the main verb forms and tenses used at Level Two are:

- common irregular forms of past simple verbs, *going to* (for prediction and to state intention) and common phrasal verbs
- modal verbs: *will* and *won't* (to express willingness) and *must* (to express obligation or necessity).

Also used are:

- adverbs: irregular adverbs of manner, further adverbs of place and time
- prepositions: of movement, further prepositions and prepositional phrases of place and time
- adjectives: comparison of similars (*as . . . as*) and of dissimilars (*-er than, the . . . -est in/of, more* and *most . . .*)
- conjunctions: *so* (consequences), *because* (reasons), *before/after/when* (for sequencing)
- indirect speech (statements).

Specific attention is paid to vocabulary development in the Vocabulary Work exercises at the end of the book. These exercises are aimed at training students to enlarge their vocabulary systematically through intelligent reading and effective use of a dictionary.

To the student:

Dictionary Words:

- Some words in this book are darker black than the others. Look them up in your dictionary or try to understand them without a dictionary first, and then look them up later.

Laura,
and

People knew the two girls by their family names, Banford and March. They lived on Bailey Farm together. They were the only people on the **farm**.

Banford was small and thin. She was often ill and wore glasses. March was stronger than Banford. March did most of the work on the farm. She worked with her hands and made things. The girls were not young or old. They were about thirty. And they wanted to do well on the farm.

But things were not easy. They had a lot of **chickens** on the farm. March made nice houses for the chickens. The chickens had beautiful homes. March made hot food for the chickens. But the chickens did not eat well and were often ill. March worked with the chickens early in the morning and late in the evening. There was no time to read or go for a walk. March wore men's trousers and moved **like** a man. But her face was not a man's face. She had dark hair and big dark eyes. There was something unusual about her. Sometimes perhaps she was dangerous.

There was danger on the old farm. A **fox**! The fox ate the chickens. Again and again. The girls tried to kill the fox. But the fox was too quick for them.

Banford and March were usually best friends. But sometimes they didn't speak for two or three days. Banford was ill but warm at the same time. March did the work. And there was always more work. Now and again there was an angry fire in March's eyes. Then Banford was afraid of her. And March spoke angrily to Banford.

The fox made the girls angry. They looked for him every morning and every evening. Sometimes they saw his head or his **tail**, but they never caught him.

Suddenly March saw the fox quite near her. He looked up at her and she looked down into his eyes.

One evening in August March was outside with the chickens. She watched the chickens and thought about everything and about nothing. She had the gun under her arm. The trees were beautiful in the sun.

Suddenly March saw the fox quite near her. He looked up at her and she looked down into his eyes. The fox looked at her and he knew her. She did not move. The fox knew her and was not afraid. Then the fox turned and ran slowly away. He jumped over something and then he was gone, like the wind.

March walked after the fox.

'I must find him,' she said.

She walked and walked. She did not find the fox. She went slowly back to the farm.

Banford talked to March at dinner. March said little. She did not tell Banford about the fox. Then she stood up and took the gun again. She went out to look for the fox.

One evening later that week March suddenly said to Banford: 'The fox was at my feet on Saturday night.'

'Did you kill him?' Banford asked.

'No,' March answered. 'It was very sudden. He wasn't afraid of me.'

They did not talk about the fox again. But the fox was always with March. The fox lived in her head. Weeks and months went past. It was soon autumn. It was dark by four in the afternoon. Banford and March did not like the dark.

One evening the girls sat together by the fire. It was dark and wet outside. Banford looked into the red fire. Suddenly both girls looked up. They heard something. There was somebody outside. They waited. They heard somebody by the door. The door opened. Banford jumped.

A man's **voice** said quietly, 'Hello.'

March took up the gun.

'What do you want?' she asked angrily.

Then a young man walked into the kitchen.

Again the man's quiet voice said, 'Hello.'

Then a young man walked into the kitchen.

'Who lives here?' the young man asked.

'We live here,' March said. 'What do you want?'

'Oh, I'm looking for William Grenfell,' the young man said.

'He doesn't live here,' March said.

'Oh. William Grenfell is my **grandfather**. He lived here. I lived here five years ago, too,' the young man said. 'Where's my grandfather?'

The young man was about twenty. He had a round face and long, light brown hair. His eyes were blue. He was wet and had a hat in one hand. He looked at March with the gun in her hand.

'We came here three years ago,' Banford said. She was not afraid now. 'There was an old man here before.'

'He's dead then,' the young man said.

March looked at him. To March he was the fox. She looked at the young man and saw the fox.

'You didn't know about your grandfather,' Banford said.

'No,' the young man answered. 'I was in Canada. I went there four years ago. I came back last week.'

'Do you want to sit down?' Banford asked. 'Do you want some tea?'

'Yes,' he said, and sat down. 'The house is different.'

'You can see it's not the same as before,' Banford said.

March was in the kitchen. She cut bread and made tea. She thought about the young man. She brought the food into the room and put it on the table. She did not want the young man to look at her. She went back into the kitchen.

Banford talked to the young man. She was very happy. She liked talking. She talked to him like a brother. Banford called to March.

March came back into the room. She took her tea and sat in the corner of the room. It was dark in the corner. The young man could not see her there. The young man ate all the bread. March cut more bread. Banford talked and talked. The young man asked questions about the farm. From time to time he looked at March in the corner. His eyes came back to her again and again.

'I came to this farm when I was twelve years old,' the young man said. 'I lived here with my grandfather. But I wasn't happy. So I went to Canada and worked there. Now I'm back.'

He asked the girls more questions about the farm.

'We don't only think about work, you know,' March said suddenly. 'We don't want to work all day like animals.'

'We want some time to think and talk,' Banford said.

The young man laughed.

'You want a man on the farm,' he said. He laughed again. The girls laughed, too.

Then Banford began to ask questions. The young man's name was Henry Grenfell. No, he was not called Harry, always Henry. March sat in the dark corner of the room and watched the young man. He was the fox and he was here in the room with her. She was happy in the dark corner.

'The fox can't see me,' she thought. 'But I'm near him.'

Soon it was late in the evening. They stopped talking. The young man looked round.

'Well, I must go,' he said. 'I must find a place to sleep.'

'Perhaps you can stay here,' Banford said. 'But . . .'

'What?' he asked.

'But what are the people in the village going to say?' Banford said. 'Two girls and a man in the same house? What do you think March?'

'The village can think what it likes,' March said. 'It's not important to me.'

6

March sat in the dark corner of the room and watched the young man. He was the fox and he was here in the room with her.

March put her hand out to the fox.

'Well,' Banford said. 'You can stay the night.'

The young man smiled.

'Thank you very much,' he said.

Banford made a room ready for him. To her he was like a brother. The girls went to bed together.

At midnight March opened her eyes. There was a sound outside the house. It was the fox.

'The fox is singing,' March thought. 'I can see him.'

March put her hand out to the fox. He was very yellow. Suddenly he turned and ran away. His tail hit her face. It was hot, like fire. March slept again.

In the morning the young man ate breakfast with the girls. Then he went into the village. He came back to the farm in the afternoon.

'What am I going to do?' he asked the girls.

'What do you **mean**?' Banford asked.

'Where am I going to find a place to stay?' the young man said. 'There are no rooms in the village.'

Then he stopped speaking. He waited quietly. Suddenly he looked at March. She saw his blue eyes. They were hot like fires. They were like the eyes of the fox.

'I don't know,' Banford said. 'What do you think, March?'

March said nothing. The young man's eyes were on her.

'Go on, say something,' Banford said.

'What can I say?' asked March.

'Say what you think,' Banford said.

The room was quiet. The young man's eyes were like strong lights.

'He can stay here,' March said.

'I think he can, too,' Banford said.

'Thank you very much,' the young man said. 'You're very good.' He smiled.

One or two days went past and the young man stayed on

the farm. Banford liked him very much. He helped with the farm work, but not too much. He liked to go out with the gun. He liked to kill animals. He liked to watch things. He often watched March. She was new to him. Her eyes were exciting. He liked her words.

It was evening. He was outside in the dark. He saw the lights of the fire in the farmhouse. He liked the farm. Suddenly he thought, 'I want this farm. I want March. I want March to be my wife. I want to **marry** her. Why not? She's a year or two older than me. That's OK.' He thought of her eyes and smiled.

Now he didn't know what to do. He was afraid of March. He was afraid to speak to her. She was like an animal. And he was like a fox. But he did not know how to get her.

It was two weeks later. It was a cold dark afternoon. The young man was outside. March was with him. They did farm work together. The young man looked at March.

'March?' he said in his quiet young voice.

She looked up at him.

'Yes?' she said.

'I want to ask you something,' he said.

'Do you? What is it?' she said. She was afraid.

'What do you think it is?' he asked.

March looked into the young man's eyes.

'Well,' he said very, very slowly and quietly. 'I want to marry you.'

March turned her face away. The young man was like a fire. Then, very suddenly, she spoke.

'You don't know what you're talking about. I'm older than you. I'm as old as your mother.'

'I do know what I'm talking about,' he said quietly. You're not as old as my mother. How old you are is not important, and how old I am is not important. Years are nothing.'

'Well,' he said very, very slowly and quietly. 'I want to
marry you.'

She listened to his quick, quiet words. She closed her eyes. 'I can't answer,' she thought.

'I want to marry you, you see,' he said again quickly. He waited for her answer. She was very near him and he wanted her. But he waited.

'Say,' he said. 'Say you're going to marry me. Say it.'

'What?' she asked. Her voice was very quiet. He was very near to her.

'Say yes.'

'Oh, I can't,' she said. 'How can I?'

'You can,' he said, and put his hand on her hand. 'You can. Yes, you can,' he said, and very slowly put her hand to his mouth.

'Don't!' she said. She opened her eyes and looked at him. 'What do you mean?'

'I mean what I say,' he said again. 'I want to marry you. I think you know that now. You know that.'

'What?' she said.

'Know,' he said.

'Yes,' she said. 'I know you say you do.'

'And you know I mean it, too,' he said.

'I don't know what I know,' she said.

'Are you there?' Banford called from the house. 'Come in. The food's ready.'

March and the young man went into the house.

'Is something wrong?' Banford asked.

'No,' the young man said.

Banford was quite angry with Henry. But she did not know why. She did not like to look at him. She did not like his eyes or his face. He was too hot, too strong.

The evening was very quiet. Henry usually read, or walked round the farm. He liked to walk at night and listen to the sounds of the night. Tonight he sat in a chair and read.

*Banford was quite angry with Henry. But she did not know why.
She did not like to look at him.*

In her head she heard the fox singing. 'There he is!' she said and stood up quickly.

Banford looked at his long brown hair. She did not want him in her nice room. The room was clean and warm with nice chairs. The young man was not right in the room. March sat at the table. Banford sat in a small chair with a book.

'Oh,' Banford said. 'My eyes are bad tonight.' And she put her fingers to her eyes.

Henry looked up but did not say anything.

'Are they?' March said.

Henry began to read again.

'What are you thinking about?' Banford asked March.

'What?' March said. In her head was the sound of the fox singing.

'What are you thinking about?' Banford asked again.

'Nothing,' March said. 'I'm thinking about the sound of the wind.'

Banford began to read again. She was not thirty years old, but some of her hair was white. Henry turned his eyes to March. She had a warm light face. She looked down at the table. In her head she heard the fox singing.

'There he is!' she said and stood up quickly.

'Is something wrong?' Banford asked. 'Who's there? Do you mean Henry?'

'Perhaps,' March said. She didn't want to talk about the fox.

At nine o'clock March brought in some bread and milk and tea. Banford drank some milk and ate a little bread.

'I'm going to bed, March,' she said. 'I'm tired tonight. Are you coming?'

'Yes, I'm coming,' March said. 'In a minute.'

'Don't be long,' Banford said. 'Good-night, Henry.'

'Good-night,' he said.

Banford went out of the room.

'Come and sit down a minute,' Henry said quietly.

'No, I'm going. Banford's waiting,' March said.

'Why did you stand up five minutes ago?' Henry asked.

'Oh,' she said. 'I thought you were the fox.'

'The fox? What fox?' he asked quietly.

'One evening last summer I saw a fox. The fox was near me and I saw his eyes,' March said and turned her head away.

'Did you kill him?' Henry asked.

'No,' she said. 'He looked into my eyes and then ran away with a laugh on his face.'

'A laugh on his face!' Henry said, and he laughed, too. 'And you were afraid of him?'

'No, not afraid,' said March. 'But I remember him.'

'And you thought I was the fox,' he laughed.

'Yes,' she answered. 'For one minute.'

'Answer my question,' the young man said. 'About marrying me.'

'No,' March said. 'I'm going. Banford is waiting.'

'Is it because I'm like the fox? Is that why?' Henry laughed again.

March turned and looked at him. He stood up and walked up to her.

'Stay for a minute,' he said quietly. He put his hand on her arm. She turned her face away from him. 'Am I like the fox?' he asked quietly.

March tried to move but his strong arm stopped her.

'Answer my question,' Henry said. He **kissed** her face quickly. He tried to pull her to him.

Then March heard Banford's voice.

'Banford's coming,' March said.

When she spoke he kissed her on the mouth with a quick warm kiss. It was like fire.

'Marry me,' he said.

'March! March! What are you doing?' Banford called from the bedroom.

16

He put his hand on her arm. She turned her face away from him.
'Am I like the fox?' he asked quietly.

'Say yes,' said Henry.

'Yes! Yes! Anything you like! Anything you like! I must go,' March said. 'Banford's calling.'

He moved away from her and she ran out of the room.

◆

The next morning at breakfast Henry spoke to Banford.

'Do you know what?' he said.

'What?' asked Banford.

'Can I tell her?' Henry asked March.

March's face turned red.

'What is it?' asked Banford. Her face was tired.

'March and I are going to marry,' Henry said with a smile.

Banford put down her knife. She looked at March.

'You what?' she said.

'We're going to marry, right, March?' Henry said.

'You say that we are,' March said. Her face was very red.

'Never!' Banford said and stood up. 'It's not right.' She was angry and afraid at the same time.

'Why not?' Henry asked.

'She can't marry you,' Banford said. 'She doesn't know you.'

'Yes, she does,' Henry answered angrily.

'I see,' Banford said. 'Perhaps she knows you too well.'

'What do you mean?' Henry asked. 'I don't understand.'

'Perhaps you don't,' Banford said. 'I don't want to talk about it.'

Banford took the bread and tea out to the kitchen. Henry sat angrily at the table. He was like a big, red, angry child. He did not speak to March. Then he stood up. He took the gun and went out. He came back for lunch and then went out again. In the evening he sat angrily and did not say much.

Later that night Henry was in bed. He listened to the

18

'Never!' Banford said and stood up. She was angry and afraid
at the same time.

'I'm going to die,' Banford said. 'He wants me to die.'

sounds of the farm. The night was quiet. He heard a fox far away and then a dog. Then he heard Banford and March.

Henry got out of bed. He walked quietly to the door of the girls' bedroom. He stood outside the door and listened. It was cold and dark.

'I'm going to die,' Banford said. 'He wants me to die. Then he can live here with you. I can't live in the same house as him. I don't like his red face. I can't eat my food when he's at the table.'

'Well, he's only here for two more days,' March said.

'Yes,' said Banford. 'Good! I don't want to see him again. All he likes is to go out with the gun. You don't know what you're doing. He's not going to live here.'

'No, he isn't,' March said.

'But he thinks he is,' said Banford. 'That's what he wants. He wants to live here. No, he's not coming here.'

'We can tell him that he can't live here,' March said.

'Oh, yes,' Banford answered. 'I want to say a lot of things to him. I don't like him. He's not good for you. You don't understand him.'

'I don't think he's as bad as all that,' March said.

Banford began to cry. March talked to her quietly. Henry walked slowly back to his bedroom.

He got into bed. It was difficult to sleep. He got up again and dressed. It was quiet. He went down to the kitchen. He put on his coat and took the gun. He went outside. He walked slowly away from the house.

'Perhaps I can kill the fox tonight,' he thought. He stopped and waited.

He waited a long time under the dark trees. Then the fox came. He saw it near the chicken house. The gun was in his hands. He killed the fox. The women heard the sound of the gun. March opened the bedroom window.

Henry took the dead fox by the tail and showed it to March. The fox was beautiful. March did not know what to say.

'Who is it?' she asked.

'It's me,' Henry answered. 'The fox is dead. I killed it.'

Henry took the dead fox by the tail and showed it to March. The fox was beautiful. March did not know what to say. She went back to bed. When she was in bed, she cried.

In the morning March and Banford looked at the fox. His tail was red and black. March put her hand on the fox's thick tail. She looked at his ears and black nose. She looked at the fox's long, white teeth. He was beautiful. And he was dead.

'He's good. Do you like him?' Henry said.

'He's a good, big fox,' March answered. 'He killed a lot of my chickens.'

'Is he the same fox?' Henry asked.

'I think he is,' March answered.

In the evening Banford asked Henry, 'When are you leaving?'

'The day after tomorrow,' Henry answered.

'What are you going to do then?' Banford asked.

'What do you mean?' Henry said.

'About March,' Banford answered. 'When are you going to marry her?'

'I don't know,' Henry said.

'When is March leaving?' Banford asked. 'You can't live here with her.'

Henry looked at Banford. 'I don't know,' he said.

Banford laughed.

'I'm going back to Canada,' Henry said.

'And taking March with you?' Banford asked.

'Yes,' Henry answered.

March looked up. 'Canada?' she said. 'You didn't say that before.'

Banford looked at March. 'So you're going to Canada?'

'Perhaps we can marry first,' Henry said. 'And then go to Canada.'

March looked at him. 'I don't know,' she said slowly. 'I want to think about it.'

'Why?' Henry asked.

'Because I want to,' March answered.

Henry was angry. He didn't know what to do. March and Banford stood up.

'We're going to bed,' March said. 'Good-night, Henry. I'm not coming down again tonight.'

Henry sat by the fire. He wanted to marry March. He did not know why he wanted her. But he did. He wanted to go to Canada with March. And the next day was his last day on the farm.

In the morning Banford went into the town. She went to the shops and bought things. She came back in the afternoon. She walked to the farm from the train station.

Henry watched Banford. She had a lot of things in her arms. Henry did not like Banford. He did not go and help her with the things. He stood and watched her.

Then March ran out to Banford. Banford stopped and waited for her. March took all the things from Banford. She carried everything. All Banford carried was some yellow flowers. Henry could see the women, but they could not see him. He could hear them.

'Can I help you?' Banford asked.

'No, thank you,' answered March.

'Are you angry with me about Henry?' Banford asked. 'Because he can't stay here?'

'No,' said March.

'I don't understand why you like him,' Banford said. 'You're too good for him. I don't know what you're doing. It's a mistake. He's going to be a bad husband.'

'No,' said March. 'I know what I'm doing.'

Henry listened to the women. He did not like Banford.

24

*Henry did not like Banford. He did not go and help her with
the things. He stood and watched her.*

*Henry looked at March again. His mouth opened. He did not know
what to say. She was different.*

But he liked March more and more. He wanted to see her tonight. He wanted her in his arms. He wanted her near him. Henry thought about March for a long time. Then he went into the house. He saw the two women in the kitchen. It was time for tea.

Henry looked at March again. His mouth opened. He did not know what to say. She was different. She did not have trousers on. She had a pretty green dress on.

'Why are you wearing a dress?' Henry asked

March smiled. 'Because I want to,' she said.

Henry looked and looked at March. He did not see Banford. He forgot her. He ate his bread and drank his tea. And he looked March up and down, up and down. March went over to the fire and got more tea. Henry watched her. When she moved he saw her legs and feet. She had a short skirt and black shoes. She was a beautiful woman and he wanted her. He wanted her for his wife.

The evening went on. March did not say very much. At nine o'clock they had more tea. Henry waited for Banford. He wanted Banford to go to bed. She was usually the first to go to bed. But tonight she sat and read. Sometimes she looked at the fire. Nobody said anything.

'What time is it?' March asked quietly.

'Five past ten,' Banford said.

'What about bed?' March asked.

'I'm ready when you are,' Banford answered.

'All right,' March said. 'I'm going to get things ready.'

March went up to the bedroom. Banford did not move. She listened carefully. March came down again.

'There you are, then,' she said. 'Are you going up?'

'Yes, in a minute,' said Banford. She did not move.

Henry watched Banford like a cat. Then he stood up.

'I think I'm going out. Perhaps there's another fox out

there,' he said. 'Come with me March. Let's see what's out there.'

'What! Me?' March said suddenly.

'Yes. Come on,' he said. 'Come on for a minute.'

'It's late at night,' said Banford. 'It's too late to go out.'

'Only for a minute,' Henry said.

March looked from Henry to Banford. Banford stood up. 'It's too cold. Too cold and too dark,' she said.

'She can have my coat,' Henry said angrily to Banford. 'You're coming,' he said quietly and warmly to March.

'Yes, I'm coming' she answered and turned away.

Banford started to cry. She put her hands on her face and cried. March looked back from the door. Henry had his hand on March's arm.

'No,' he said and put his coat round her.

'I must,' March said. 'I must go to Banford. I must.'

'Wait a minute,' he said 'Wait a minute.'

'She's crying her **heart** out,' March said.

'Her heart,' he said. 'What about your heart, and my heart?'

'Your heart?' March asked.

'Yes,' Henry said. 'Isn't it as good as her heart?'

'Your heart?' March said again.

Henry took her hand and put it on his heart.

'Yes, my heart! Do you think I haven't got a heart? There's my heart,' he said.

Henry's heart moved under March's hand. She did not know what to do. She forgot Banford. Henry's hand pulled her outside.

'Come with me,' he said warmly. 'Come out and talk. Let's say what we must say.'

He closed the door and they went out into the dark.

They sat on a box outside the house.

Banford started to cry. She put her hands on her face and cried.

'Give me your hand,' he said.

She gave him her hand and he put it between his hands.

'You're going to marry me,' he said. 'You're going to marry me before I go back to Canada. I've got a good job there. It's in a nice place near the mountains. Why not? I want you. I want to be with you.'

'You can find another girl,' she said. 'There are a lot of girls in Canada.'

'Yes,' he said. 'But I want you.'

They sat in the dark. They did not say anything.

'I don't know what to do,' she said. 'I don't know what I want. I don't know anything.'

'You want to be with Banford,' he said. 'You want to be in bed with her.'

She waited a long time before she answered.

'No,' she said. 'I don't want that.'

'When I am old,' he said. 'I want you to be with me.'

March laughed. 'I can't think of you as an old man.'

'Don't laugh at me,' he said.

'Why not?' she asked.

'Because I want to talk to you,' he answered.

She said nothing. Then she said, 'No, I'm not laughing at you.'

His heart was hot. 'So you're going to marry me before I go to Canada.'

'Yes,' she said.

'There,' he said. 'That's it. Let's go in. It's cold.'

They stood up.

'Kiss me first,' he said.

He kissed her slowly on her mouth. It was a young, quiet kiss. Then they went in.

Banford was by the fire.

'So you're here,' Banford said angrily. 'You were a long time.'

She gave him her hand and he put it between his hands.
'You're going to marry me,' he said.

The next day Henry left. March was at the station when his train left. She watched Henry leave.

'Yes, we talked about things,' he said. 'We're going to marry as soon as we can.'

'So that's it. I hope you're not making a mistake,' Bancroft said.

'I hope so too,' he answered.

'Are you going to bed now, March?' Banford asked.

'Yes, I'm going now,' March said.

March looked at Henry. His eyes were on her. She wanted to be with him. She wanted to be his wife. Henry looked into her eyes.

'I remember your words,' he said. 'I remember what you said. We're marrying at Christmas, and going to Canada in April.'

March smiled and went to bed.

The next day Henry left. March was at the station when his train left. She watched Henry leave. She thought of Henry's eyes. She thought of how his nose moved when he laughed.

◆

Nine days later Henry got a letter.

Dear Henry,

I think about you and me all day. But we can't marry. When you are here all I see is you. When you are away I can think better.

In my heart I don't know that I love you. I want to be open with you. I don't see why I'm going to marry you. I don't know you well. I know Banford ten times better than you. She's not well. How can I leave her?

It's all a big mistake. I can't go to Canada with you. I'm sorry. I can't marry you. Please forget me.

Banford's mother and father are staying here at Christmas.

March

*She started to cut the tree down with an axe. Banford and her
mother and father came to watch.*

Henry's face was white and angry when he read the letter. He took a bicycle and left quickly for the farm. It was a hundred kilometres. The weather was cold and wet.

At the farm March was outside. She was by a big dead tree. She wanted the tree for the fire. She started to cut the tree down with an **axe**. Banford and her mother and father came to watch.

'Be careful,' Banford said. 'The tree is going to hit the chicken house.'

'No,' said Banford's father. 'It's not going to **fall** near the chicken house.'

March started to cut the tree again. It was difficult.

'Look, there's somebody on a bicycle,' said Banford's father.

'Who is it?' asked Banford's mother.

March looked. Her face went red. She knew. But she did not say anything. The bicycle came nearer. It was Henry. His face was wet and red. Henry spoke to Banford's mother and father. March did not move. Henry was the fox. Her mouth opened. It was all finished. She knew he had her now.

'March is cutting down a tree,' Banford said.

'Here, give me the axe. I can finish it for you,' Henry said.

March gave the axe to Henry. He took off his coat.

'Is it going to fall on us?' asked Mrs Banford.

'No,' said Henry. 'But look at those chickens!'

There were four chickens under the tree. Banford ran after the chickens and the chickens ran away. She stopped ten metres from the tree. Henry looked at Banford. 'The tree is going to fall and hit her,' he thought. He looked again. In his heart he wanted her to die.

'Be careful,' he said. 'The tree is going to fall there.'

'No, it isn't,' said Banford. 'I know what I'm doing. Cut the tree down!'

She looked up at him. Her face was wet. He knew that he had her now. He was happy.

Henry took the axe. He cut quickly into the tree: one . . . two . . .

Slowly the tree turned and fell to the right. Banford stood there. She made a small sound when the tree hit her and then fell. The back of her head was red. Her legs moved and then stopped. Henry and March ran up to her.

'I'm afraid she's dead,' Henry said quietly.

March's face went white. She looked at Henry. Then she started to cry. She cried and cried like a child. After a long time Henry took her hands. She looked up at him. Her face was wet. He knew that he had her now. He was happy. He wanted her, and now he had her.

But he did not have all of her. They married at Christmas. Then they left the farm and started for Canada. March loved Henry. She wanted to be his wife. But she was not happy. Something important was not there. There was nothing for her to do. All there was to do was to be with Henry. Henry wanted to make her his woman. His woman and that was all.

Henry and March walked by the sea. They looked out across the sea to Canada.

'Things are going to be better for you in Canada,' he said.

She looked at him. Her face was like a tired child's.

'Perhaps,' she said. 'I don't know.'

EXERCISES

Vocabulary Work

Look back at the 'Dictionary Words' in this story. Do you understand them all now? Write seven new sentences with these words in them:

a voice/like
b grandfather/farm
c axe/chicken
d kiss/marry
e heart/mean
f tail/fox
g tree/fall

Comprehension

1 Look back at the pictures and answer these questions.
  a Picture 1 (page 2) What time of day was it when March first saw the fox?
  b Picture 2 (page 4) Who does the young man say he is looking for?
  c Picture 7 (page 14) Is the fox really singing? What can March hear?
  d Picture 9 (page 19) Why is Banford angry?
  e Picture 11 (page 22) What does March do after she sees the dead fox? Why?
  f Picture 13 (page 26) Why is March wearing a dress, not trousers?
  g Picture 15 (page 31) Why do you think March is afraid to marry Henry?
  h Picture 18 (page 36) Why is Henry happy?

2 Who said this? Who to? Where?
  a (page 3) 'The fox was at my feet on Saturday night.'
  b (page 18) 'Never!'
  c (page 21) 'I'm going to die.'
  d (page 28) 'There's my heart.'
  e (page 37) 'I'm afraid she's dead.'

38

3 When and where did these things happen in the story?

  a March first saw the fox.

  b Henry first met Banford and March.

  c Henry first thought 'I want March'.

  d Henry first asked March to marry him.

  e Henry and March first kissed.

  f Henry killed the fox.

  g Henry watched Banford carry the shopping.

  h Banford died.

Discussion

1 March wanted to stay with Banford and not marry Henry. Was she right?

2 At the end March is unhappy: 'There was nothing for her to do. All there was to do was be with Henry.' Why was she unhappy?

3 March thinks of Henry as the fox. Do you know people who are like animals?

Writing

1 Write a short letter from Mr Banford to the police about how Banford died.

2 Henry and March go to Canada. One year later March writes a letter to Mr and Mrs Banford. Write March's letter in 100 words.

Review

1 Which part of the story did you enjoy most. Why?

2 What do you think about Henry? Is he nice? Or did he mean to kill Banford?

3 How important is the fox to the story? Can you retell the story without the fox?